# A Question Of Gin

The Scottish Alchemists

Disclaimer:
The authors of this book have presented the most accurate information to their knowledge at the time of writing. This book is intended for discussion purposes only. The authors do not imply any results to those using this book, nor are they responsible for any results brought about by the usage of the information contained herein.
No part of this book may be reprinted, electronically transmitted or reproduced in any format without the express permission of The Scottish Alchemists.
Published by The Scottish Alchemists
Copyright © 2020 The Scottish Alchemists
All rights reserved.
ISBN: 9798572724653

Since March 2020, The Scottish Alchemists have had the most well-informed and irreverent gin podcast out there. This book is your chance to join in the Alchemists' chat with questions from different episodes of their podcast.

With over one hundred questions, this is an infusion of provocations from all the episodes of their entertaining podcast. Challenge friends and family or play in teams to use this book as a pub quiz. Use at your gin society or book club with gin instead of literary inspiration. Or simply use the questions as conversation starters. Like gin, enjoy responsibly.

You can follow The Scottish Alchemists on Instagram, Facebook and Twitter. Listen to their podcast on iTunes and Spotify. Contact them by email at TheScottishAlchemists@gmail.com

# DEDICATION

To Juniper – thanks for the memories

## Contents

**JOYCE'S GINVENTORY ............................................. 1**

**CAROL'S CHEMISTRY CORNER ............................. 7**

**JENNI'S GINSPIRATION ....................................... 13**

**21 DAYS OF GIN .................................................. 19**

**DO YOU KNOW SCOTTISH GIN? .......................... 23**

**CHEMISTRY CORNER ANSWERS ......................... 27**

**SCOTTISH GIN ANSWERS .................................... 31**

**ABOUT THE AUTHORS ........................................ 35**

The Scottish Alchemists

# ACKNOWLEDGMENTS

Thanks to our Manager of Technical Content for helping to get our podcast across the airwaves ....and for his cheeky commentary of each episode.

The Scottish Alchemists

## JOYCE'S GINVENTORY

1. Brand Ambassadors come in all shapes and sizes – if you were a distiller with your own gin what type of person would you like for your brand ambassador?

2. Everybody has a different palate and preferences. What gin suits you and you like that doesn't suit your friends and they absolutely don't like?

3. If you could invent a gin that tasted like your favourite food or meal what would it be?

4. In 2020 two of The Scottish Alchemists attended an exclusive private gin tasting at Habibi Gin in Vienna. What capital city, and gin from that country, would you like to experience a private gin tasting in?

5. During early 2020 a video of Stanley Tucci making a Negroni went viral. If you could have anybody alive or dead to make you a cocktail – who would it be and what cocktail would you get them to make you?

6. We've had a unique Brockman's gin cocktail with a bit of tablet (a very sugary Scottish sweet) in the bottom of the glass. What type of sweet would you fancy finding in the bottom of your gin cocktail?

7. There are endless amounts of food and cookery shows on TV at the moment and a tasting on one was hot cross bun flavoured gin. What are your thoughts on gins that taste like cake?

8. Anno Gin is 95% ABV – what's the highest ABV gin you've ever had?

9. At Easter time some people make Easter egg cocktails – alcohol in a chocolate easter egg. What other type of edible 'container' would you use to make a seasonal gin cocktail?

10. During the Corona Virus lockdown months, lots of people have not been able to go to pubs or bars to enjoy gin. What's your favourite bar for gin?

11. There are lots of Instagram gin accounts which now double up with other interests and hobbies e.g. Gin and Blooms or Gin and Seeds. If you had to add another area of interest or another of your hobbies to your gin account, what would you add – Gin and what?

12. There are lots of 'alcohol free spirit' drinks on the market at the moment. What do you think makes a spirit a spirit?

13. Biggar Gin launched their Biggar Strength gin during lockdown. Launching a gin during lockdown could be seen as a high-risk strategy – what could the advantages or disadvantages be of launching a gin at this time?

14. One mum on Instagram was using gin miniatures as a home-schooling activity with her children to get them to make a gin advent calendar. This ticked lots of curriculum boxes. What else do you think you could do with gin which would cover different areas of the school curriculum?

15. There has been a rash of online virtual drinks events and distillery tours which appeared over the timespan of the Corona Virus. Do you think they will still remain relevant once the lockdown restrictions are over?

16. There are lots of virtual tasting companies who repackaging distillers' gins in their own miniature bottles with their own branding. How would you feel about that if you were a distiller?

17. There are some beautiful boxed sets of gin and two glasses. What's the nicest boxed set you've ever seen?

18. If someone was to ask you to choose a gin for your best friend's birthday, which gin would you choose for them?

19. Alchemist Joyce enjoys a gin while relaxing in the bath. What gin would you choose to enjoy in a luxury bubble bath?

20. Is there anything a gin distiller or brand ambassador could do that would make you not recommend their gin, even if it tastes incredible?

21. There is a huge amount of social media accounts related to gin. What do you think are the differences between a ginfluencer, a blogger and a blagger?

22. Tweed Valley Distilling Company give a percentage of their profit from Meldon Dry Gin to Tweed Valley Mountain Rescue Team. If you had your own gin who would you give a percentage of your profits to?

23. There are some stunning bottles out there for gin at the moment. If you were to invent a gin of your own, what type of bottle would you go for?

24. Our habits and timings changed during Covid-19 lockdown and we all got into different routines. What's your favourite and most regular time of day to have a gin?

25. Gin and lemonade or gin and water – discuss.

26. Botanicals are normally listed on the back of a bottle of gin or on the distillery or gin website. Do you like to know the botanicals and read the reviews before you drink a new gin, or do you like to figure out the taste?

27. Alchemist Joyce sometimes has a big meal before a gin drinking session. She likes a 'liner' to line her stomach before serious gin activities. What food you do you like as a 'liner' before you start drinking?

28. Gins of the world – name a gin from as many different countries as you can.

29. There are Gin Awards all over the world, with the usual standard categories. If you were to run your own Gin Awards, what categories would you have?

30. The makers of Norfolk gin play music when they are making their gin. How many songs or tunes can you think of with a gin or a distillery in the title?

# CAROL'S CHEMISTRY CORNER

1. Name the main botanical found in gin?

2. Some juniper is native to the UK, but the best is found in which of these 3 countries – Cyprus, Turkey, North Macedonia?

3. In a 70cl bottle, approximately what mass of juniper berries, in grams, does it contain?

4. Name the botanical root that is used to fix the flavours in gin – hint, the forename of a famous actress with the surname Huston.

5. Angelica root is used by the people in Finland to make a musical instrument called what?

6. Cassia root is also used as a botanical in gin, which other well know spice is it closely related to?

7. Which chemical compound is the major component in the oils of both juniper and coriander?

8. Gin is based on which alcohol? A bonus point for the chemical formula.

9. Above what alcohol percentage (alcohol by volume ABV) does the spirit need to be before it's classed as a gin?

10. There is spirit based drink that can be classed as a gin even though it contains less than 37.5%ABV alcohol, can you name it?

11. Highly concentrated ethanol can be used as the basis for gin production; it is called neutral grain spirit (NGS), what % ethanol does it contain?

12. Tonic water contains a chemical which helps prevent malaria, can you name it?

13. What is an *illuminating* property that quinine possesses?

14. Quinine comes from the bark of which tree?

15. Which class of chemical compounds does quinine belong to (hint: a Glaswegian alcoholic)?

16. Which of these is closest to the quantity of quinine in tonic water? 50mg/l or 100mg/l or 500mg/l?

17. Gin is produced in stills traditionally made from which metal?

18. What is the chemical symbol for copper?

19. Quinine comes from the cinchona tree. Where does the cinchona tree originate?

20. What colour is fresh or polished copper metal?

21. What type of compounds are removed by the copper in the still which would taint the gin with "farty" odour?

22. Pot stills used in the distillation of gin are also called what?

23. The pot still has a long slender tube which comes out of the top - what's it called?

24. Some stills have a vertical distillation column to allow finer separation of the liquid - what other name is given to this column?

25. Gin can be made by a compound or bathtub method - what does this mean?

26. What is the minimum ABV for a Navy strength gin?

27. The USA use a measurement of proof relating to the alcoholic content of a gin. If a gin has an ABV of 50%, what's its proof?

28. Which part of the distillation mixture is desired and collected to make gin?

29. To the nearest 5 million, how many bottles of Bombay Sapphire are produced each year?

30. Which UK distillery has the tallest rectification column at 18m high and contains 60 plates?

The Scottish Alchemists

# JENNI'S GINSPIRATION

1. What are the ingredients lurking at the back of your kitchen cupboards that you'd chuck in a cocktail?

2. Smoked rosemary is one of my favourite garnishes – what's your "go to" garnish?

3. Early podcast guests were Double Dutch Drinks – does the tonic you use make a difference to your G & T?

4. The Alchemists love a breakfast gin, what's the earliest you've had a cheeky wee libation?

5. Black Tomato gin is often referred to as a marmite gin – you love it or hate it. What gin do you love that's a bit "different"?

6. Harris Gin bottles famously make good lamp bases. Have you ever made anything out of an empty gin bottle and if so what?

7. If you're having a wild house-party do you buy lots of cheap gin or a few bottles of good gin?

8. How many bahookie glasses have you got? And if you don't have any of these, what glass do you prefer to drink your gin out of?

9. Our nibbles of choice, to drink with gin of an evening range from Branston Pickle Cheddars and olives through to Cadbury fruit and nut and tablet. What's your gin nibble of choice?

10. Thinking of accompaniments, what's the strangest thing you've ever been served with gin?

11. Alchemist Jenni is very partial to making her own syrups – is it worth the faff?

12. There have been lots of new gins launched during 2020 at various price points - have you bought a newly launched gin this year?

13. We've done photoshoots all over the place – beaches, garden trees etc. Our favourite are the blue dresses on the beach – what's your favourite Alchemist shot?

14. Straws – discuss! Consider:

    a. Cocktails and G & Ts
    b. Paper
    c. Sustainable/eco friendly
    d. Other uses

15. Non-alcoholic gins are a No-No in the Alchemists' book but for what occasion or whom you would spend £25 on a bottle of flavoured water?

16. The Scottish Alchemists have hosted gin tasting events in all sorts of places including a health spa – what are the health giving qualities of your favourite gin?

17. Alchemist Jenni is a fan of Aviation gin and Ryan Reynolds. Do you have a favourite celebrity endorsed gin?

18. Who would be your ideal guest on a gin podcast?

19. Alchemist Jenni's infamous nano batch gin is Tadger's Hole – what would you call your gin?

20. The gin Alchemist Jenni buys over and over again is Lone Wolf – what's yours?

21. What gin have you spent a lot of money on that was just "meh"?

22. The Scottish Alchemists have drunk gin all over the world – what's the most exotic or far flung place you've had gin?

23. The Scottish Alchemists don't often have guests on the podcast but if you came on what would be your specialist subject – and don't say gin!

24. Alchemist Jenni glazes over at times during Carol's Chemistry Corner but do you like to know all the ins and outs of how gin is made?

25. Alchemist Jenni is often inspired by the enthusiasm and passion of distillers – have you met anyone in the gin world who has inspired you?

26. Seeing all the gin collectors and enthusiasts on social media with huge gin collections – whose gin collection would you raid?

27. If you've ever been to a trade show like Gin to My Tonic or on a distillery tour have you then spent an inappropriate amount of money on gin because you were just a little bit tipsy?

28. If you could have a job in the gin industry what would it be?

29. If you had a gin still which you could name, what would you call it

30. How much does a pretty bottle influence what you buy?

31. The Alchemists often use colloquial phrases. What is 'wreck the hoose juice'?

32. Why was gin once known as Dutch Courage?

33. The Scottish Alchemist enjoy a good drink while we record the podcast :
    a) Can you tell?
    b) Would you like to be able to go to work and have a wee drink?

The Scottish Alchemists

# 21 DAYS OF GIN

1. A gin which is your all-time favourite

2. A gin with a bottle which could make a good lamp

3. A gin you'd buy if you had an unlimited budget

4. A gin you'd take to a house party

5. A gin with a number in its name

6. A miniature gin you'd smuggle into a concert

7. A classy Scottish gin

8. A gin to persuade the non-gin drinkers

9. A gin you've been gifted and you'd like to regift?

10. A gin you are embarrassed to like

11. A gin for a cold winter's day

12. A gin cocktail

13. A gin you would buy to impress

14. A gin which is at least navy strength

15. A gin with a romantic story

16. A gin you enjoyed in a foreign country

17. A gin with a colour in its name

18. A gin that reminds you of someone you'd rather forget

19. A gin you want to like but don't

20. A gin for a hot summer's day

21. A gin to celebrate the end of Covid-19 lockdown.

The Scottish Alchemists

# DO YOU KNOW SCOTTISH GIN?

1. How many gin distilleries are there in the small Scottish town of Peebles?

2. Achroous Gin is distilled by which company?

3. Makar is a gin made in Glasgow. What does Makar mean?

4. How many types of 1881 gins are available in December 2020?

5. Milk Thistle is one of the main botanicals in a well-known west coast Scottish gin – which one?

6. The Highland Liquor Company makes which elegantly bottled gin?

7. Which Scottish gin was designed for and supports the darts community?

8. Where in Scotland is The Hendrick's Gin Palace?

9. Meldon Dry Gin is named after two hills local to the Peebles area. What elite fighting force of their day is also associated with The Meldons?

10. Which gin describes itself as 'Made in a bar, not a boardroom'?

11. Which gin distillery is based at The Secret Herb Garden?

12. The Lone Wolf range of gins is made by which famous brewery?

13. Name one of the three gin distilleries on the Orkney Isles?

14. The Botanist is distilled on which Scottish island?

15. Mr Mackintosh is the pet at which northernly Scottish distillery?

16. Which gin comes from the Isle of Jura?

17. Beinn an Tuirc distillery makes which range of gins?

18. Who was the Master Distiller responsible for Tobermory gin?

19. Isle of Skye's "Tommy's gin" was named after whom?

20. Oro gin produced in the Dalton distillery is in which part of Scotland?

21. Which island distillery has recently produced their latest batch of gin from their newly commissioned still named after their daughter who was born during lockdown 2020?

22. Eidyn Gin is a collaboration between whom?

23. One of Arbikie's gins is called Kirsty's Gin – who is Kirsty and what is her surname?

24. Hill and Harbour and Galloway Gin is made in a distillery located near Newton Stewart. What is the name of that distillery?

25. Seaglass Gin is made by which Distillery, where?

26. Which distillery has named their still 'Ugly Betty'?

27. Which gin is made in the former 'Dick Vet School'?

28. Which micro pub serves Scottish craft gin on tap through a microscope?

29. Which distillery uses water from Loch Ness for its gin?

30. Rule Gin is made by Bloodline Spirits following in the footsteps of their forebearer Andrew Usher. What was Andrew Usher famous for apart from the Usher Hall in Edinburgh.

# CHEMISTRY CORNER ANSWERS

1. Juniper berries

2. North Macedonia

3. 30-35g

4. Angelica

5. A fadno – a reed type instrument

6. Cinnamon

7. Linalool

8. Ethanol (a bonus point for the chemical

formula $C_2H_5OH$ )

9. Above 37.5%

10. Sloe gin

11. 95-96%

12. Quinine

13. Fluorescent under UV light

14. Cinchona tree

15. Alkaloid

16. 100mg/l

17. Copper

18. Cu

19. South America : Venezuela, Bolivia, Peru etc

20. red/ orange/ brown

21. Sulfates

22. Alembic

23. Swan neck

24. Rectification column

25. Steeping botanicals in NGS/ethanol without further distillation -

26. 57%ABV

27. 100 proof (The UK proof was 1.75xABV)

28. Hearts

29. 40 million

30. BrewDog Lone Wolf distillery

# SCOTTISH GIN ANSWERS

1. Three – 1881 Distillery, Tweed Valley Distillery (Meldon Dry Gin), Rule Gin

2. Electric Liquor Co.

3. A poet or bard

4. Five – London Dry, Pavilion Pink, Subtly Smoked, Navy Strength, or as they were rebranded Hydro, Honours, Pavilion and Rafters. Tiffin Gin was available in a small batch of 100 bottles.

5. Glaswegian

6. Seven Crofts

7. Double Trouble

8. Girvan

9. The Knights Templar

10. Porters Gin

11. The Old Curiosity Distillery

12. Brew Dog

13. Deerness Distillery, Orkney Gin Company, Kirkjuvagr

14. Bruichladdich Distillery, Islay

15. Dunnet Bay Distillery

16. Lussa Gin

17. Kintyre Gin

18. Stephen Woodcock

19. Tommy Wilson who was the father the distillers

20. Lockerbie, Dumfriesshire

21. The Isle of Barra Distillers Co.

22. Aldi and the Old Curiosity Distillery

23. Master Distiller Kirsty Black

24. Crafty Distillery

25. Deerness Distillery, Orkney

26. Bruichladdich Distillery, Islay, makers of the Botanist

27. Pickerings in Edinburgh – the Dick Vet School was the Veterinary College in Edinburgh

28. Rutherfords in Kelso

29. House of Elrick

30. He is known as 'the father of blending' because he perfected the blending of Whisky producing the famous Usher's Green Stripe and Old Vatted Glenlivet. Founder of the North British Distillery Company.

The Scottish Alchemists

# ABOUT THE AUTHORS

What do a former Banker, a Chemistry Teacher and a business owner have in common? Yes, the answer is gin!

While gin did not bring them together it's certainly taken their friendship to a new level. As The Scottish Alchemists Jenni, Carol and Joyce started hosting gin tasting events in 2018, before making the successful transition to podcasting in March 2020. While face to face events, where they are able to share their passion for gin, is still their favoured format - this book, supported by the podcasts, takes them to a whole new audience.

Printed in Great Britain
by Amazon